The Comfortable Garden

Designs for Harmonious Living

The Comfortable Garden

Designs for Harmonious Living

Ann & Scot Zimmerman

Sterling Publishing Co., Inc. New York
A Sterling/Chapelle Book

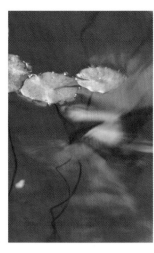

Chapelle, Ltd.:
- Owner: Jo Packham
- Editors: Ray Cornia, Caroll Shreeve
- Staff: Areta Bingham, Kass Burchett, Jill Dahlberg, Marilyn Goff, Karla Haberstich, Holly Hollingsworth, Susan Jorgensen, Barbara Milburn, Karmen Quinney, Cindy Stoeckl, Kim Taylor, Sara Toliver, Desirée Wybrow
- Proofer: Laurel Ornitz
- Photography: Scot Zimmerman

If you have any questions or comments, please contact:
Chapelle, Ltd., Inc., P.O. Box 9252, Ogden, UT 84409
(801) 621-2777 • (801) 621-2788 Fax • e-mail: chapelle@chapelleltd.com
website: www.chapelleltd.com

Library of Congress Cataloging-in-Publication Data

10 9 8 7 6 5 4 3 2 1

Published by Sterling Publishing Co., Inc.
387 Park Avenue South, New York, NY 10016
©2002 by Ann Getz Zimmerman and Scot Zimmerman
Distributed in Canada by Sterling Publishing
c/o Canadian Manda Group, One Atlantic Avenue, Suite 105
Toronto, Ontario, Canada M6K 3E7
Distributed in Great Britain and Europe by Cassell PLC
Wellington House, 125 Strand, London WCR2 0BB, England
Distributed in Australia by Capricorn Link (Australia) Pty. Ltd.
P.O. Box 704, Windsor, NSW 2756, Australia
Printed and Bound in China
All Rights Reserved

Sterling ISBN 0-8069-6413-8

Scot Zimmerman

Scot Zimmerman is a photographer specializing in architectural interiors and exteriors. He is the sole photographer for four books, *Romanza, the California Architecture of Frank Lloyd Wright*; *A Guide to Frank Lloyd Wright's California*; *The Details of Frank Lloyd Wright*; and *Frank Lloyd Wright, the Western Work*. His photographs also have been featured in more than twenty other books, many of them published by Chapelle, Ltd./Sterling.

Ann Getz Zimmerman

Ann Getz Zimmerman writes about art, architecture, and interiors for *Salt Lake Magazine* and *Utah Style & Design*, and is a free-lance contributor to numerous regional and national magazines. She and her husband Scot travel the country together on assignments, and base their business from their Victorian farmhouse in alpine Heber City, Utah. This is her first book collaboration with Scot.

Michael Glassman, Technical Advisor

Michael Glassman has designed hundreds of landscapes, earning him professional groups' highest awards, television and radio appearances, and the expert's role in *Sunset* magazine and numerous other national publications. He studied landscape design at the University of California and La Napoule Art Foundation in France.

TABLE OF CONTENTS

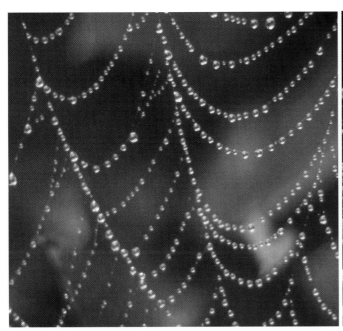

Introduction

What is it about a garden that allows us to breathe deeply, relax, and forget about our problems? Many gardens are works of art, creating an environment of tantalizing colors, textures, and scents, but only certain gardens beckon us outside to truly enjoy ourselves and relax.

What makes these gardens especially comfortable for us? Could it be the way they stimulate our senses? Visually, the shapes and color varieties please us. The spicy scents awaken us to the surprises of nature, and the sounds of water, breezes, and ringing wind chimes make us aware of the constant changes in the natural world. In this age of ecological awareness, we are ever more conscious of our reliance on and connection to nature.

Recent trends in architecture and interior design point to uniting the outside with the inside and making our gardens living spaces. Whereas once landscapes were intended more to frame the exterior of the home, the landscapes of today invite us outside to take pleasure in our surroundings. Our yards are alternative outdoor rooms of our homes, offering places to sit, eat, wander, and enjoy.

In seeing these outdoor spaces as rooms, many of the same principles hold for comfortable gardens as for good architecture and interior design. We discover rhythm, motion, variety, texture, harmony, color, and contrast. Spots of rest and quiet balance active areas, and there should be a sense of scale and symmetry. Anticipating human movements through the space, we arrange items for ease of touch. Colors are coordinated, and structural as well as decorative materials are selected carefully for comfort and durability. How we live in the space is taken into consideration, so we bear in mind lighting, both sunshine and artificial light. These outdoor spaces are configured for compatibility and comfortable transitions from one to another. Thus, it is not surprising that some people now call landscaping "outdoor architecture."

The outdoor room (left) beyond the sliding glass doors in this home becomes part of the interior through the clever use of repeating materials. The tiles and their mortar pattern make a smooth transition from interior to exterior. The rows of support posts, the wall of glass offering a view in both directions, and the ceiling ribs of the patio echoing the roofline inside pull both spaces together.

This covered patio (right) plays up the vertical siding. Mirroring post supports accent where path meets patio. The foliage makes a transition to the patio through the use of spikey grasses in country-theme containers. The graduated heights of the foliage and the white posts carry our eyes upward to merge the outer garden, the patio, and the tree branches for an engaging room effect.

In creating a comfortable garden, the true genius lies in also considering the demands of the living things outdoors. For each plant, there must be proper soil, moisture, drainage, and light. You need to think about plant blooming cycles and heights at maturity when combining plants, for the overall effect of the garden as it progresses through the seasons. Wise gardeners time the opening of blossoms, coordinate the textures of the leaves, balance the heights of the plants, and anticipate the seasons, so that there is always something to enjoy.

As an art form, architecture seeks life and movement in the inanimate. Adding living plants to the creative palettes of architects and designers emphasizes the passage of time and the transitions through growing cycles. In the garden, you are much more aware of the sun's movement through the day and how its position affects light and shadows as the seasons progress. Plants proclaim the seasons in buds, blooms, and the peaking and waning intensities of their foliage colors. Plants show the play of shadows in movement from the wind and display the drama of new and ever changing life.

The comfortable garden lures us outside and away from the things that preoccupy us elsewhere. It must have a sense of place and a scale that is perfect for us. The gardens shown in this book accomplish all of this through their well-thought-out design, composition, lighting, plantings, and hardscape. Delightful walkways and stairways lead us through the foliage, to meet up with porches, decks, and patios, or garden shelters like gazebos, cabanas, and greenhouses. These gardens can be lively places or refreshing refuges for people, as well as wildlife.

Just as a comfortable home protects us from the elements, gardens need to provide shade, shelter, and security, in addition to privacy. Similarly, as we add art or design themes to interior rooms, we can enhance the garden with collections that reflect our interest in certain hobbies or pets, or horticultural preferences for particular bulbs and flowers, perennial beds, or favored annuals. Finally, all interior design plans include furniture and wall-space considerations. In a comfortable garden, the starting point is design and composition. This garden is truly personal and unique.

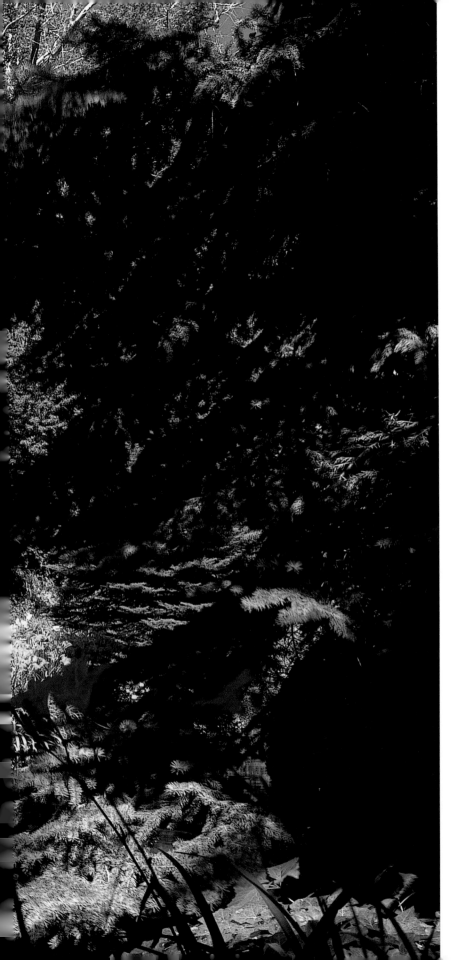

The gardens we have selected show ways of including flowing water, fountains, and ponds. Water features add sensory elements to a space by cooling, providing delightful soothing sounds, and supporting aquatic plant and animal life.

Swimming pools can be incorporated into gardens, and this book offers new ways to consider them as part of your living space instead of a separate feature in the yard.

The key to a comfortable garden is creating an atmosphere in which the plantings and the constructed features work harmoniously together, to become the place you seek out for relaxing, meditating, and celebrating life.

Chapter 1

Design & Composition

In creating a comfortable garden, we want to design a place where we can be in touch with nature and take a break from life's demands. It should be a place to regroup in solitude or to celebrate with family and friends.

The first step is to tune in to your values to decide what is truly important to you. Perhaps you already understand your needs. To be certain, explore public parks, buildings with well-landscaped grounds, the gardens of friends, and those featured on garden tours. What appeals to you most?

Consider relationships of sunshine to shade, water elements, drama, and whimsy. Do you want to include entertainment spaces, hidden getaways, or places to recline or sit up high with a pleasing view? Study large open spaces, canopies, and gazebos, too. Trigger your comfort awareness by walking through your own home, registering what pleases you and why. Your home expresses your taste. Borrow its flair for your outdoor plan. Remember your dreams of returning to a certain vacation spot. Incorporate its sensory detail and restorative qualities to make your own outdoor environment just as desirable.

If you lack experience and confidence as you attempt to design a permanent garden space for the first time, take a cue from this homeowner's versatile approach to creating an outdoor room.

Dry-stacked stones have been used here as low walls and paths to define a shady, private seating area. The high-walled wooden fence shuts out distracting noise and hides views of the surrounding neighborhood or encroaching shopping and traffic areas.

Combinations of perennial planting beds and containers of blooming annuals create a lush established atmosphere to complement the mature evergreen that acts as a ceiling for this outdoor room. Note how the fence and the tree are the only immovable elements of the design.

If living in the space gives you better ideas for accommodating other activities, the dry stones can be restacked into different configurations. It is advisable to rework the area after the growing season, when disturbing roots will be less of a problem. Many plants could be moved in their containers and others relocated nearby with their earth-protected root balls intact. Path stones could be shifted to change walking directions or widened with more rows of dry stones to create a patio under the tree. Also, the stone bench, echoing the dry-stacked wall, can be moved to a more desirable location.

This narrow side-yard challenge is beyond the skills of most homeowners, and would be best undertaken by design and construction experts. In a neighborhood where there is little leeway for lot line legalities and privacy, let alone charming focal points, the beauty and function of a lap pool and pergola-style shelter have transformed a problem situation into a stunning activity area. Every inch of space, from foundation to retaining wall, has been exploited and lit in the most dramatic fashion. The rock wall fireplace at the street end of the covered patio is a visual destination for swimmers and a literal privacy maker and sound barrier from traffic passing by at the front of the home. The people traffic, by comparison, flows easily from inside through the French doors, onto the patio, and into the pool, or along the foundation-hugging walkway that borders it.

Moving into the interior of the patio room for closer appreciation of the ambience-creating details, the flagstone floor with its basket-weave pattern has been repeated in the fireplace facing. The bold architecture is emphasized by the scale of the fireplace, which appears from the pool view to complete the water expanse visually with a finishing wall of a similar width to the pool. This accounts for the asymmetrical placement of the fireplace on the pool side of the patio, rather than centering it on the end wall. The lighting of the ceiling beams and pergola slats neatly closes the box of the room with an upper-level pattern of openwork that reflects the floor rectangles. The low garden retaining wall is an extension of the floor and continues out into the garden, running along the pool wall in an unbroken and pleasing visual line.

These Japanese gardens are perfect examples of symmetrical beauty, created through purposeful selection and placement of natural and man-made elements. The tori gate flanked by stone lanterns frames a path and foliage vista leading to deeper space (this has spiritual connotations, as well). The brilliant red gate symbolizes good fortune.

It not only commands the space as a focal point, but it is also the traditional Japanese entry announcement for a sacred temple. Visitors approach on a simple path, conceived to free them to meditate appropriately on the way. A Japanese garden is not an assembly of themed garden accents. Rather, its goal is always simple beauty, taken to the abstract in a calming, restful space of any size.

In Japanese gardens every detail is designed to echo life cycles in nature. The simplicity of the bamboo-and-stone fountain has been so thoughtfully planned out that, when the flow of water arches to the stone basin below, the bamboo spout and the receiving stone bowl are visually linked by the third element of the water itself. The circle thus formed by the supporting rod of the spout has a balance that is literal as well as spiritual.

The gifts of each earth element are connected in the circle of life. Trees, here represented by the bamboo, not only take their sustenance by way of the water but also give it back to the earth, symbolized by the stone.

Though rocks are one of nature's most stable entities, over time humble water can wear them away. The lesson provided is one of patience and interdependence of all things.

The sunlight, a fire element, is the power force that makes the water flow or freeze. All are interdependent and connected.

Achieving the timeless quality so apparent in the artistry of Japanese gardens requires great sensitivity and restraint.

Chapter 2

Paths, Stairways & Bridges

*P*aths, stairways, and bridges allow us to see, gain access, and therefore come to appreciate all that gardens have to offer. They link the areas of the garden and lead us from one to another, uniting such features as entries, patios, gazebos, pools, shade gardens, planting beds, fountains, fish ponds, and garden art. The magic, however, comes from how creatively these paths are designed to draw us away from daily concerns, as we leisurely walk through an ever-changing garden setting.

Just as architects and interior designers plan for function, accessibility, and the experience of moving through our homes, we need to devote similar attention to the details of outdoor spaces. And when these details are achieved with a level of style and functionality, they allow casual meandering or restorative strolls down the pathways, up the stairs, or over the bridges in any outdoor garden.

Where paths or stepping stones are situated is determined by the area, the elevations, and the ease of accessibility to every part of the garden. Many details need to be taken into account when planning and constructing a path. Primary paths should be wide enough for wheelbarrows, mowers, the occasional transport of a portable grill or tent, wheelchair access, and so forth. Even such practicalities as reaching the compost pile must be accounted for in pathway design. Paths should be made of materials that allow for every shoe type, from sneakers to high heels. Safety must also be considered, so deep puddles, uncovered roots, or eroding embankments should be minimized or eliminated. Considerations for lighting, both natural and electric, at levels from underfoot to above the head of the average visitor, must be included in an overall plan, as should the inclusion of hand rails and the levels of risers for stairs.

Both long- and short-term plans for walkways are advisable. Put in the features and materials you can afford as you progress toward your fully realized design. A pathway defined by pine straw, shaved bark, or gravel can suffice until you can afford flagstone, river rock, or brick. Make improvements and upgrades as gently as they occur in nature, if possible. This way, no matter what wonderful new idea is being implemented, it will not impede the accessibility to a favored garden area for very long. The sense of quiet comfort in nature should remain throughout all construction transitions, whenever possible. Then, as your garden evolves with maturing plants and seasonal changes creating a timeless elegance, so can the accessibility features of pathways, stairs, and bridges be improved and augmented.

The unifying idea with all of the pathways in these gardens is their established timeless quality.

The dry-stacked stairs (above) are especially unique, because their risers were constructed by using the slab stones on their edges vertically. The terraced flower beds curving into the steps are retained with low, dry-stacked stone walls. All elements curve upward and abut one another in a textured, rustic rhythm, providing a fine example of variety-within-unity design.

This wide three-step stair arrangement (upper left) is repeated after a path proceeds to the next elevation. The lush foliage bordering all path and stair sections leads up visually, in anticipation of what is to come.

The steep curving stairs (lower left) on this hillside property are made more welcoming and climbable with their broad tread space. Their visual rhythm leads up to and echoes the pergola above.

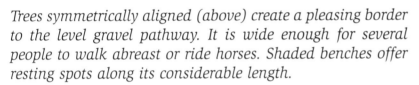

Trees symmetrically aligned (above) create a pleasing border to the level gravel pathway. It is wide enough for several people to walk abreast or ride horses. Shaded benches offer resting spots along its considerable length.

The romantic sculpture and round pool (upper right) of this formal garden are made more casual and comfortable with rustic stone paths and a minimum of classically trimmed shrubs. Rose bushes and other foliage have been pruned only enough for control, but not overly so.

This path (mid-right) skirts the foundation of a home in a slight curve. Bordered by a purposeful use of ragged forms and a strong vertical topiary, this path is not only functional but also beautiful.

Where space can appear endless, the curve of this wide, flat walkway (lower right) introduces mystery with a view-obscuring hedge.

You can make gradual elevation changes more interesting when a graded path is transformed (above) into a series of wide and deep stairs with shallow risers. As weather effects of rain, wet leaves, snow, or ice may make such grades slippery, steps may be less daunting as well. Because the tread area is broad and deep enough to allow for two people or one person with a pet, the steps are only half as high as public park stairs or those in the average home. The gentle appearance of the gradual climb is emotionally comforting, whereas the repeating risers curving into the distance creates a sense of beauty in rhythm. As the trees obscure the destination, climbing to find out what lies around the bend lends a sense of mystery and anticipation.

Paths allow us to observe, while the scenes of nature unfold and change. Changing our orientation to different views of the garden that play up these attributes is achievable through the creative design of paths, stairways, and bridges. Try walking many times through your yard, in many different directions, at various times of the day, and in different seasons. As you do this, a plan will start to take shape in your mind for where to place the most practical and aesthetic viewing points. Gardeners should devote time and thought to this process before the selection of materials and the construction ever begin, because without this assessment and envisioning process the garden's delights will not be fully realized.

This stone path across a pond in Japan inspires garden planners to create their own alternatives to bridges across shallow-water features. Can you imagine the enjoyment children and adventurous adults would have in stepping or hopping from one raised step to another? Such a beautiful spot would call for a pause now and then to watch the flash of a koi fish or to study the delicate blooms of water lilies.

You can be a bit more adventurous in your design plans for secondary paths. They can take the garden visitor along a wall, beside a stream, or through an archway that opens onto a shady rest stop. Perhaps with only stepping stones to lead the way, a secret path to a child's special playhouse could be designed.

These varied walkways determine order in the garden's many sectors. They lead us to spacious gathering areas for groups and intimate resting stops for conversation, without breaking the harmony at any point. Getting there should be half the fun and returning should ease the visitor's transition from retreat spot to busy world.

Smooth transitions of path width, the right selection of materials, and the integration of plants, lighting, elevations, stairs, bridges, and other features may take a few seasons of trial and error.

It is easy to understand why it's as important to consult a landscape designer as an expert who will lay the pipes for your hot tub. Do not underestimate the practicality and the aesthetics of pathway, stair, and bridge planning.

Chapter 3

Fences, Trellises & Walls

*I*t is undecided whether or not fences make for good neighbors, although walls and fences are basic boundary elements in most gardens. They keep out the neighbors' dogs and in the country deter wandering deer and escaped livestock. However, to achieve a sense of comfort, any garden should feel protectively enclosed but not confined. We need to find a balance between celebrating the freedom of nature and providing privacy and protection from noise, interruptions, and uninvited guests, be they animals or people.

Whether walls add to or detract from the comfort of your garden depends on how they support the overall plan in function and harmony of design.

In country-garden settings, we expect to see a picket fence as a backdrop for well-established perennials. Its historic charm lends a nostalgic note to even a first-season country-theme garden.

The structure of your home or your regional location will play an important role in establishing the theme or the style of your fence. Fence materials, design, and height considerations need to be integrated purposefully. Plan to harmonize your fence with existing buildings, elevations of terrain, and special features you want to be able to see from different vantage points. It's also important to consider the physical and emotional ramifications of the fence on family members and visitors. Decide whether you want to see through the fence or over it. Will people sit on the fence, or is it used only as a theme accent? Are the rails supposed to keep pets and children inside, or have they been constructed to support climbing roses or to form a graceful transition from an archway to a patio?

Pattern, shape, and theme are design elements that imaginative homeowners look for in fence construction. They may use rough-hewn logs to create a feeling of rustic Western charm or antique found art to carry out an old-world theme. An old gate rehung in a new fence has a certain nostalgic appeal. You may want gates meant to call attention to themselves as garden accents to be larger than functionally necessary. If the fence's purpose is decorative only, the spacing of posts and rails, or even their uniform style and shape, can be given a whimsical treatment. The play of delicate and bold fence patterns is more interesting when light passing through them casts their shadows onto a path, body of water, or patio. Fences as works of art invite us to enjoy details of artistry and craftsmanship unique to their materials. Wrought-iron filigree, turned-wood knobs and curves, and cast-iron leaves and flowers are but a few elements you can incorporate in your garden setting.

One of the objectives of a comfortable garden is to maintain a human scale. Trellises and arbors lower the height, delineate paths and walkways, and draw attention. Just as a hallway leads to the next room in a home, a trellis invites us to the next garden space. One of the techniques of architecture is to lead us through a low ceiling that explodes into a larger space. Trellised archways can accomplish the same effect in a garden setting (see above).

Space, affluence, and expert planning are apparent in this handsome, permanent, wrought-iron arched trellis (right). It frames a broad, concrete-block pathway approaching a set of stairs leading to a charming home. The homeowner's plan for you to enter through a bower of grapes and fragrant roses lets you know that the home will be a welcoming treat as well.

Painting a wall is the quickest and least-expensive way to transform its visual impact. Choose a contrasting color, or select colors that are harmonious with ones used elsewhere on the property. Here, by painting a mural, whimsical use is made of a neighbor's garage wall (see above). The mural calls for viewers to use their imagination to look beyond billowing curtains, out a window, to the sea.

This unusual wall (left) highlights the arid setting. A low wall painted in earth-toned colors breaks up and redefines an otherwise ordinary space. It creates interest without a need for many plants, an important consideration in thirsty environments. Even recycled water evaporates at a high rate in the desert. The two-thirds-higher wall with its asymmetrically located fountain defines another level of space, acts as a cliff for a restrained cascade, and affords privacy in a shared courtyard. It is high enough to sunbathe without being observed and at the same time low enough to see out the window without looking into a wall. The walls harmonize with the native rocks, give the falling water its splashing sound, and hide the water recirculation system.

trellis to cover the wall with vines and eventually hide the structure. The creative possibilities are almost endless.

Rather than trying to disguise such a wall, another approach is to emphasize it by designing other structures to complement it (below). This aggressive wall treatment gives a dynamic thrust to the structure and divides the garden into interesting and useful sections.

Sometimes the most difficult design challenges come from existing features such as a wall (above). Rich color and found objects have transformed what was once a plain retaining wall with little interest. The contrast in size, shape, texture, and form in this casual arrangement makes a memorable focal point for the garden. Two fluted poles were leaned on either side of a diamond-hung frame to create a symmetrical triangle to steady what could have become a hodge-podge of disparate stuff.

Although this example follows the theme of outdoor collectibles, other design themes could be equally attractive using this wall. For instance, in accord with a southwestern theme, you could alter the surface of the wall using a stucco treatment to make it look adobe. Facade brick would give it a classic appearance. You could paint a mural on the wall to give the whole garden a European feeling or install a

Who says corners where walls meet have to be only functional? Here, the textured rock of this ancient-looking wall forms a visually stimulating background for a potted-plant focal point.

A curved armchair repeats the rounded forms of the walls and pottery, supporting the focal point, and invites garden visitors to enjoy the partial shade, with a good book.

Should you want to create a timeless garden setting, although the walls are new, many products and techniques can be used to achieve the look of age. Roughened stucco, facing stone, or used brick can be applied unevenly for an old-world appearance. Applying a coat of paint in a certain way can soften new edges and give the appearance of a well-used wall. To further age a new wall, use a hammer to break off sharp edges and gouge out chunks of material. Chains, chisels, crowbars, and other instruments can also give the wall a distressed patina.

Harmonize forms to balance an area design and emphasize a focal point. The round flowerpot featured on a bulbous cistern and its lid (above) prompted the home-owner to select a chair with curving elements rather than straight ones.

Low walls can solve a myriad of garden problems and add rhythmic beauty at the same time. Whether mortared or dry-stacked, such walls have rustic textures and shapes echoing themes from nature.

Perfect for retaining walls or for defining flower beds, they also lead the eye in a landscape to follow a line to see where it goes. These low walls are both graceful and practical.

Note the different top-surface treatments of the two walls to the right. The even stones (upper right) on the mortared wall tempt children to walk upon them and provide a place for adults to sit and enjoy the flowers.

This wall (lower right) is fashioned after the dry-stacked walls in Europe. Stones are stacked on top of each other and fit together like a puzzle, without mortar. Although they look temporary, they will last for hundreds of years.

The style of each wall should complement the character of the house and the garden it surrounds. A dry-stacked wall can be used to enclose a home surrounded by large open meadows of lavender or mustard plants. As seen in English-style gardens, this type of wall is also appropriate for surrounding old-world roses and hollyhocks.

46

The dilapidated roof, aging pillars, and wonderfully shabby shutters set the antiquarian theme. The classic cast bust on the window shelf and the balusters lined up beneath it add an accent of whimsy. The contrasts are guaranteed to make viewers smile.

Weathered buildings bring out imaginative decorating ideas in eclectically inclined homeowners. They seek out such properties and enjoy the challenge of incorporating a jumble of mismatched items into a pleasing ambience. The element of surprise is a vital component in this approach to garden design, but it does not override good design principles.

In the example shown at the left, the short privet-hedge wall forms a soft boundary between the wild decor of the shed and the simpler motif of the patio/lawn area. Some advantages of living foliage used as a wall are that it can repair itself through natural growth, or be adjusted in height and width by simple pruning.

Notice how this is still a very new garden (above). As the plants grow and mature, and a patina of age collects on the masonry, an added air of elegance will slowly develop.

The challenges of this design are to block out the noise and the confusion of a busy residential area and create the impression of a classic European walled garden. The outdoor-room concept is very pronounced due to the fireplace and pergola.

Many strong architectural features are the signature of this patio's design. Classic columns support a substantial pergola shelter, which is softened visually with climbing vines. Eventually it will provide shaded comfort for guests below. A paddle fan is mounted on the pergola to cool the area. The vines are being trained along the privacy fence, up and over the pergola, and across the fireplace, connecting them with enveloping foliage. The homeowners extended an existing high-wall fence with the addition of the fireplace wall. Varying the fireplace structure with three horizontal shelf levels brings the fence down into the space while also providing display areas for containers and collectibles.

There are ways to add variety to what could otherwise be a monotonous wall. During the design and construction phase, stagger wall heights, vary the foreground height, or create triangles, arcs, or curves. The owner of the home (below) used plants to form tiers of foliage to accent the walls and the elevations of the house. The selected plants and the graduated levels of the stone walls add color and texture to the overall design of the property.

The massive Royal palm trees and the symmetrical stair and wall treatments are undeniably stately. Although all elements have been orchestrated to lead to an impressive entry, little attention has been given to people's comfort in gathering in outdoor living spaces, as there are none! This is an excellent example of design, color, texture, harmony, and scale that ultimately ignores human comfort, until you are invited inside.

Chapter 4

Porches, Decks & Patios

Porches, decks, and patios often become the focal point of garden designs, because many outdoor activities center around these structures. Outdoor cooking, eating, swimming, and lounging are usually tied to features especially designed to accommodate and enhance these activities. To maximize the enjoyment of porches, patios, and decks, it is important to review their intended usage and then build or adjust them accordingly. For example, if a deck is intended for dining, it should be built deeper than usual to allow for a table to be set up, while still letting people comfortably walk around it.

Another option is to combine or connect a porch with a patio or deck. These additions and combinations of porch, patio, and deck allow the garden designer to introduce various levels of living space and visual variety through a range of building materials. With the structural variety comes additional options for specific planting areas and types of foliage. A raised porch accommodates taller plants and offers protection and shade for several varieties of flowers requiring partial shade to thrive. Porches also provide ideal areas to display potted plants and collectibles.

Nowhere in the United States are front porches more celebrated than in the South; for genteel Southerners, they are a way of life. Regardless of geographic location, porches are not only an added detail to the front of the house, but the perfect place to socialize with neighbors or just relax. Some experts believe if the front porch were used more often, neighbors would be closer friends and neighborhoods would become similar to extended families.

There are as many styles of porches as there are sides to a house. You can use a front porch for welcoming guests, light conversation with family members, or reading during daylight hours. A side porch can be used for quieter times, such as an intimate dinner with close friends. For special dinner parties, lanterns can be hung and the table can be set with china and candles carried from inside. The back porch is often a more casual space and used for garden chores. It is here that corn is husked, flowers are arranged, and vegetables are stored. In the hot months of summer, children often sleep here to be cooled by the evening breezes.

The porch, whatever its purpose, should be well equipped for various activities. For instance, gardening tools and potting and flower-arranging supplies need to be at hand where we can use them. This is just as important as furniture being placed where we want to sit.

With some patios, the concept of being an outdoor room is taken to the max, as they totally enclose the space, courtyard-style. The grape arbor in the patio (above) serves as a ceiling and defines the limits of this outdoor space. Comfortable and eclectic chairs give the area a flea-market chic feeling, while the paper lanterns illuminate and decorate this unique room. This enclosed treatment accentuates another important outdoor experience: aroma. At maturity, the grape arbor surrounds people with the scent of deliciously pungent grapes. This is the perfect place for an intimate dinner party. The mosaic-tile coffee table can be set to the side, buffet-style, and additional chairs pulled up to a vintage dining-room table, set with crystal, china, and candles.

By following the literal definition of comfort in the garden, some homeowners extend their indoor living space to the outside.

In a climate that is temperate year round, a bed can be made on the porch, so that sun and views are enjoyable in a completely tranquil setting. An outdoor bed is versatile and inexpensive, and it will be used often. A constructed wooden base supports a foam pad that quickly dries after a rain. Cover it with a natural cotton sheet, and place colorful pillows just so. A deck bed is also easy to move if the mood for a new view should strike you.

In climates where the summers are hot, but you still want to be outside, screen your covered porch with lightweight cotton panels and hang a hammock. Add a down pillow, a good book, and a pitcher of raspberry lemonade, and the afternoon is ready to be enjoyed. This arrangement is private as well as cool, no matter what the angle of the sun.

In the hot summer sun, cotton panels will fade or discolor quickly. Be prepared to replace them yearly. It is possible, however, to buy inexpensive cotton fabric and sew simple tabs across the top so panels can be threaded onto a bar.

This deck (above) shows the effect of arranging an out-door room complete with soft chairs and casual floral arrangements. The human scale created by the deck and its furnishings contrasts with the splendid view and openness of the woodsy garden. The warmth and comfort level of the space is heightened further by the vibrant red color of the tables and chairs, the scattering of throw pillows, and the easy-care decking.

Generally, only those who live in a home indicative of a Western life-style decorate with rustic elegance. This is a rugged existence, where hard work is rewarded with easy living on the porches and patios that surround the ranch house. The furniture in these outdoor living areas must be durable enough to withstand harsh climate changes and sturdy enough to hold the robust men who work the ranch. To add another element of western imagery, the bridge and porch railings here were designed the height of the wagon wheels which were attached at regular intervals. Geraniums, which bloom from spring through the short summers into the fall, are hardy choices for heavy wooden crates that won't tip over in strong summer winds. The tepee in the background is not only the perfect focal point for the deck view but is also used by children and adults who like to sleep outdoors along the river running through the property.

The patio (left) is a perfect example of excellent design combined with innovative ideas. The tall lattice fence masks out a high-density residential community. This allows visitors in the garden to focus on the beauty created by the raised terra-cotta-lined flower beds, fountains, and traditional desert plantings. The neighbor's garage wall mural has been included in the garden setting with a seascape view. The plaza atmosphere created could be Mediterranean, southwestern, or Mexican in theme.

In stark contrast to the concept of an enclosed outdoor room is this high-desert patio (above). The theme here is one of a protected oasis. The low walls discourage desert critters from wandering into the pool area, yet the view remains unobstructed. In this case, the house provides shade for afternoon enjoyment of the patio, and the pool ensures constant refuge from the heat and hydrates the living-space air. Recycled water in the fountain enhances the emotional power of water in the desert setting.

Chapter 5

Garden Shelters & Gazebos

Garden shelters and gazebos protect us from wind, rain, and sun, letting us enjoy our gardens whatever the weather. In designing the ideal refuge, you need to take into consideration the activities unique to you and your family. A garden shelter is a perfect place for conversation and sharing intimate moments, as well as for solitary hobbies like keeping a journal, writing letters, needlework, fly-tying, or making models. At the same time, it should provide scale and style for its environment.

Any garden-shelter style or design can be open, partially enclosed, or completely surrounded by screened or windowed walls and roofing of some sort. If outdoor entertaining is a high priority for you, it is wise to build an outdoor room that can be used regardless of the time of year or the weather. If your reason for building such a shelter has more to do with your personal needs, then this is the time to incorporate creativity with practicality in your design. For example, if you live in the city, where backyards are nonexistent and neighbors close, you can create a separation between yourself and your neighbor with a latticed shelter, which also offers refuge from the sights and sounds of the city.

Garden shelters and gazebos should follow already established design themes. The Japanese theme in this pavilion borrows shingled and tiled roof treatments from the home, while strong vertical uprights echo the nearby pine trees for a harmonious blend of motif, terrain, and foliage. Aging wood stains suggest the timeless tranquility basic to Japanese landscapes. The path leading to quiet Japanese garden sanctuaries can be seen as a metaphor for life's journey, forever turning, yet always simple and uncluttered.

When a property offers some variety in elevation, mature plant life, and a water resource, for sculpting a natural-feeling setting, the homeowner who can manage to finance such a grand scheme will be rewarded with memorable occasions spent with family and friends.

In this example of garden landscaping, it is interesting to note that part of the property contains a Native American burial ground, which by law must be left in its natural state. Adhering to these covenants, the pool was built incorporating natural foliage and landscaping into its design. Rocks were used as waterfalls to fill the pool with water, and the bottom of the pool was formed with polished river rocks in place of concrete or tile. This area is now not only a private and beautiful retreat, but it is also respectful of the rituals and heritage of those who inhabited the land before.

This gazebo perched above a rockwork pool is a perfect setting for adults to gather for drinks, snacks, and conversation, while keeping an eye on children playing by the shallow pool. It offers a satisfying blend of nature and landscaping.

The rockwork pool, with its two waterfalls and overhanging rocks and plants, suggests a favorite mountain swimming hole and reflects the informality of the home's foothill setting. The gazebo not only serves as a focal point for the garden and the view from the home, but its shelter increases the use of the refreshing pool.

With this pond, the water recirculation system has been incorporated cleverly into the design. Fish and water plants appropriate to the geographical region help keep the mini ecosystem healthy and the recycled water fresh, with a minimum of chemical additives.

A gazebo is the perfect structure for designing details that reflect our interests and life-style. This homeowner is fascinated by the constellations of the stars in the sky and studies everything that concerns the heavens. Thus, he built a gazebo for his garden that is a classic pillar-and-domed design, replicating the observatories for celestial research. To make it as enjoyable for other family members, he placed it at the head of a man-made stream filled with large flat rocks to create mini cascading waterfalls. He then surrounded both the structure and the stream with favorite plants that add the colors of red, orange, and yellow for the sun during the day, and shades from white to blue for the stars at night.

For just such a night, this loving wife moved the bed (above) from the bedroom to a private area in the backyard. She made the bed with a feather mattress, 600-thread-count cotton sheets, a down comforter, and lots of pillows. She then hung paper Chinese lanterns to softly light the night sky and ordered a fantastic dinner for two to be delivered and left at the front door, so that she and her husband could enjoy it quietly in bed. This truly extravagant temporary setting took a little time and some planning, but in the end it was well worth everything that the fantasy scene required.

Victorian or cottage-style lattice gazebos (upper left) with elegantly turned post handrails provide a stage for fantasy, whimsy, and playfulness. To further the theme, you can add garden furniture with a graceful curve, elegant pots and planters, and paper lanterns to this nostalgic raised-platform structure. For an occasion such as an anniversary taken to a whimsically outrageous limit, something truly eccentric might be perfect.

Both elegant and practical, this portable gazebo (upper right) can be moved about the garden. A roll-up laminate dance floor avoids high-heel-shoe and turf challenges. Move the gazebo around to alter patterns in the flow of visitors to the garden. Create shade with leaf or fabric swags, vines, and translucent paper laced into place with ribbons. When the weather turns inclement, store all the collapsible components and decorations.

You might want to try out a temporary gazebo to determine how large a permanent structure you will need for your life-style and where best to locate it. You will also be able to see for yourself the advantages and disadvantages of an open-air structure. It is possible that then you will find a screened gazebo or even an enclosed patio more to your liking.

Chapter 6

Outdoor Kitchens

A hundred years ago, summer kitchens and outdoor cookhouses were part of people's everyday living. By separating the kitchen from the rest of the home, they reduced the risk of fire to wooden-frame houses and the wood-fired stove did not heat up the interior rooms. Fifty years ago, the backyard barbecue became a staple for outdoor entertaining. Since then, grilling has evolved beyond the basic meals of hot dogs, hamburgers, and steaks, to become a type of specialty cuisine.

With this interest in specialty foods from the grill, we are drawn increasingly to outside cooking. However, today's benefits are much broader than those of a hundred years ago. Now, as outdoor living becomes more established and we are creating new spaces, guests gather on the patio and deck near the pool or backyard fountain. There, they enjoy the landscape and the escape to the outdoors. Outside living spaces offer more room to entertain. When the weather is glorious, no one really wants to be indoors; neither do they want their host to be inside, away from the fun and conversation.

Given today's life-style, the demand for outdoor kitchens is a natural progression, bringing food preparation to the place we want to be. Our yards and gardens have become retreats for us. Talented gardeners and landscapers have transformed their yards into places to be enjoyed—places that nurture and revitalize us. We live separated from nature much of the day, longing to be outside in the sunlight and fresh air. For many, cooking is a social time, so why not enjoy it with family and friends outdoors? Our featured kitchens, designed by Davis, California, landscape architect Michael Glassman, will give you an idea of your options.

Outdoor kitchens can expand a small home, so that entertaining the extended family or large groups is possible without going through a remodel of the house.

By working with a kitchen and outdoor architect, every detail of an outside cooking area can be easily realized, but not always inexpensively. Kitchens are one of the most costly rooms in the home, and an outdoor kitchen incurs many of the same costs, if not a few more. In planning your outdoor kitchen, you need to take into account the life-style of your family. The personal wants and needs of those preparing the meals must be considered as well. Informal cookouts for friends and more formal dinners when entertaining clients have their own special requirements in terms of equipment and organization. If possible, the flooring of the outside cooking area should be a continuation of that of the kitchen inside. The bar unit that contains the cooking appliances should be as near the kitchen as possible to keep steps back and forth to stock the outdoor kitchen to a minimum. To add privacy or block an unwanted view, you may want to design a large natural fireplace. Not only will it serve as a visual screen, but it will also add warmth, light, and ambience, and you can use it for roasting hot dogs and marshmallows.

Consider installing a gas grill with rotisserie for ease in cooking specialty items; a regular charcoal grill for cooking good old-fashioned hamburgers; a warming oven; a pair of smaller refrigerators, one for drinks and one for food items; and an ice machine. A counter should be included in the plans and designed at a height that is comfortable for the primary user. Most countertops today continue to be built the same height as fifty years ago when people were shorter. Countertops should be durable, weatherproof, and easy to maintain. Drawers and cabinets with metal doors should also be installed, so that cooking utensils, dishes, glassware, spices and sauces, and other necessities can be stored outside where they will be used. Plan for a sink so that dishes can be easily washed and put away, making cleanup of the area less time consuming.

Such items and amenities, if purchased all at once, can be more than the normal household budget will allow. However, with the proper plan, these items can be added one at a time until your outdoor kitchen area matches your vision.

A full-convenience kitchen can be designed garage-bay style with an automatic, retractable door that adds efficiency and instant protection for expensive food-preparation equipment. Whether it's a sudden lake squall, a mid-western tornado-level storm, a coastal hurricane, or winter's blown-in snow, weather is not a deterrent to the cook nor does it do any damage to the kitchen. Security for the kitchen is also maintained with ease when the homeowner leaves for work or travel.

A time-saving feature is being able to leave spices and utensils in drawers and cupboards and food in the refrigerator, instead of carrying them in and out for each get-together. Note the roll-in-and-out butcher block. And aesthetics have not been sacrificed to functional needs here. The wall lanterns, the tile roof that echoes that of the home, the formal columned pergola, and the elegant textured floor, accented with a few dramatic plants, set a gracious scene to welcome guests.

Chapter 7

Water Features

*G*ardeners delight in the magic that occurs with plants from the interplay of soil, sun, and water. However, water not only helps plants to thrive, but it is nurturing for people as well. Through gentle, calming sounds, water calls us to pause, listen, and look. People are naturally drawn to the sight of pools, fountains, and streams, as well as to the soothing sounds of water. While lingering by a gurgling stream, a splashing waterfall, or a trickling fountain, we can feel the busyness of our lives eddy away for a while. Such restorative moments are the goal of the gardener.

In a comfortable garden, we are gently led to see more, sense more, and be more vitally aware of our changing environment. We become better able to express ourselves visually with confidence, as we plan new features for the garden. Though water features require careful planning because of their supporting needs for pipes, pumps, and structural considerations, their beauty is of prime importance. A visual statement is not necessarily a work of art. Discriminating design awareness is key to creating a garden with well-balanced water features.

As with art, music, and poetry, what we leave out or restrain in garden design is as expressive of our taste and sophistication as what we emphasize in location, size, and scale. A highly individualized outdoor setting that expresses who we are is truly the unique garden. And water features, above all, are indicative of our personality.

Here, the homeowner has set three large ceramic urns, with glazes akin to pots viewed inside, on a gravel square in the patio. The urns fill and overflow, glistening with water. By understating all other features to simple lines and shapes, such as the rounded rustic club chairs that repeat the chunky urn forms, this unusual fountain arrangement is the variety focal point within the harmonious whole.

Earth materials in tiles, gravel, pottery, leather, woven-plant-fiber seats on the chairs, as well as the element of water itself ground the theme in primitive simplicity. They also nestle the fountain comfortably in the spatial design of the architecture. The lack of other decorative elements keeps our focus on the fountain and the framework of the space. All jarring elements have been left out. The breeze and sounds of water move freely from the garden, through the patio, to inside spaces with a minimum of interruption. That flow is purposeful, subtle, and designed to create an unmistakably peaceful mood.

79

The placement of the water feature is of critical importance. Such features should be highlighted in a comfortable garden by being designed carefully and constructed in a place of prominence. You need to consider the natural elements and elevations in such a location and to make adjustments if necessary. For example, if the site is windy most of the time, a fountain that produces a fine mist should be avoided. The wind will cause a high rate of evaporation, or the areas downwind will be perpetually wet. In such areas, where water features would still add beauty, smaller fountains or birdbaths are better alternatives.

The design theme of the garden is established or restated in the architectural elements of the water feature. The garden below is identified clearly as classic Greek by the fountain design. Its symmetry demands simplicity of setting and perfect placement of enhancing components in the design, such as the pair of chairs and columns equidistant from the centered fountain.

Fountain structures vary in materials, shape, scale, and style. This is an area where your imagination can have full reign. They can be freestanding, wall-mounted, or contrived to appear as if they had occurred naturally in the environment. Fountains define space, act as focal points, and integrate plants with garden themes.

An array of possible water features uniquely exploits the ambience and the practical advantages of water in a variety of garden styles, from nature-in-the-wild to classical.

With tier fountains, there are two or more stacked-tier pools. The top pools are narrower than those below, so that each overflows into the pool beneath. Tier fountains tend to be used in formal settings, as they were historically in the gardens of Europe and the Middle East. As tier pools are shallow, those fountains that contain only one tier are often referred to as "bird-bath fountains."

Wall fountains consist of an ornate back plate and can contain a spout. Their basins are the shape of half a circle. In both wall and tier fountains, the pump mechanisms are hidden in the basin or the base of the fountain. Wall units are hung from heavy permanent brackets sunk deep into an existing wall or affixed to sturdy latticework. Both wall and tier fountains can be made of bronze, ceramic, or welded steel.

The scale of a fountain depends upon its relative proportion to other garden components, the theme already established elsewhere, and the intended functional uses of the fountain. No matter how generous your budget, a commanding fountain out of scale and not in harmony with its surroundings will be a disappointment. The harmony you desire only takes place when aesthetic criteria are considered in the planning and selection process.

The decisions about harmonizing sizes, shapes, colors, textures, values, and patterns in relation to the scale of the garden are best made after considering fundamental design principles. If hiring experts, you can relax. If not, visit outstanding gardens and pour over books and magazines. Look for symmetrical or asymmetrical balance, variety within the unity of the design, what is emphasized as a dominant theme or feature, and what details play a subordinate role. Radiating curves as unifying elements create interesting rhythms at various elevations.

If you borrow inspiration from the past, reinterpret it by incorporating your own sense of style in the context of your life today. Pay close attention to where lines of

fences, walls, and rows of tree trunks or pillars intersect. Decide if it's a point where you want to create excitement on purpose, perhaps with a roaring waterfall. By contrast, the intersection may seem to suggest a peaceful transition spot to pause on a bench by a pond or fountain.

Repeating water features with slight variations throughout a spacious garden can create a sense of rhythm and movement, leading visitors on a journey from one to the next. Nature's wonders are always changing, yet they remain recognizably similar through their forms and patterns. Selecting stones, plants, colors, and forms indigenous to your region will make the fountains and ponds in your garden appear more natural.

Its best to have permanent fountain constructions handled by experienced professionals. They are major undertakings and well worth the added expense, especially when incorporating great quantities of flowing water with practical as well as attractive retaining walls, which can offer seating and divide the garden. Remember, hiding all pipes, pumps, filters, and the like is basic to the aesthetics of the plan.

Ponds welcome nature's complete ecosystem of plants, animals, and nutrients to the garden. It is not necessary to go to the expense of concrete installations for ponds, because synthetic liners are available in many price ranges.

Consult a local horticulturist for a list of plants appropriate for your region. Marginal plants that grow in wet soil and aquatic varieties that grow directly in the water encourage animal and fish life to flourish. Turtles, frogs, and toads will thrive, as will certain varieties of fish, such as the popular goldfish and koi.

Maintain the proper water depth in hotter climates, or overheating will kill the plant, animal, and fish life. Change the water at least once a year, even if a filter is in use and maintained properly. After draining, scrub all exposed surfaces and rocks with a pumice stone or steel wool to remove any slimy buildup. Rinse repeatedly to remove algae and bacteria that could reestablish themselves quickly and destroy the balance of the ecosystem.

There are natural systems developed by water ecologists that treat high-algae content water biologically.

Simply stated, a water garden is a garden of plants that grow in the water. Plants selected by species for this purpose generally require a minimum of four hours of sunlight per day and should cover two-thirds of the water's surface. Water-garden plants are divided into two categories: marginal plants and aquatics.

Marginal plants are water plants that thrive in shallow water and are sometimes confined to pots, which enable them to grow better with their roots protected, while inhibiting them from spreading out of control. These plants will need occasional fertilizing and repotting, so the clarity of the water will never be that of a swimming pool.

Aquatics are plants that grow directly in the water, such as the popular water lily. Which marginal or aquatic plants to include in your water garden depends upon your geographical region. Before purchasing any water life, however, its best to consult a water-horticulture expert in your area for tips.

Water always causes some sort of transformation in the garden. It can take a previously unnoticed area and turn it into a focal point or a new discovery. If this area is off to the side or out of the way, plan a path from the main garden that leads to your new water feature. Plant transitional foliage next to the path that will hint to the visitor as to what is to come. Another option is to place containers of aquatic plants in a few spots along the path leading to your surprise water feature.

Consult your local water-horticulture expert to be sure that the plants you select will attract not only aquatic animals and birds but butterflies and hummingbirds as well.

In your design, allow for some embankment plants, both soil- and water-growing varieties, to droop their fronds into the stream to create a safe hiding and feeding place for frogs and fish.

Decorate water features like the ones on these pages with delightful details such as this stone turtle (above), metal birds and large dragonflies on copper tubing, or ceramic fish with brilliant colors.

Even antique decoys can be anchored to float on the surface of the pond, attracting migrating waterfowl to land and rest. Many will stay and nest, so do not put out food beyond what the ecosystem you have established can provide, or more birds may arrive than you care to host. And their young will remember where to come next season.

Arrange benches or rocks to make a comfortable place to sit and enjoy the views and natural life of your pond or stream.

An amazing variety of plants has been brought from all over the world that we can use to transform our outdoor spaces. To lift our eyes upward, plant rushes that grow taller than we are reaching for the sun. Their long leaves wave gently in the slightest breeze, reminding us of scenes of Egypt. The arching branches of other plant varieties dip their leaves down to the surface, returning our gaze to the water.

Aquatic water lilies grow directly in the pond water or in a side-retained, calm area of a gently moving stream. Their shapes and lovely blooms are a pleasure for garden visitors as well as for fish and frogs.

Natural materials such as stacked rocks and boulders are ideal for building backyard man-made streams or cascading waterfalls. Careful planning leads to proper placement of each rock to control the way the water flows and falls. Larger rocks tend to cause small waterfall effects, whereas medium and small stones create a flow of water over and around them that reflects the light. Water sounds become more lively if the water descends from varying heights and the stream's banks alternately narrow and widen.

To calculate whether the rocks are the appropriate size or not, compare them to the width of the stream being constructed. The largest rocks, those being used to create miniature falls, should be at least two-thirds of the space from bank to bank and should not take more than one-third of the space of the streambed from side to side. The smaller rocks (not those being used as the streambed) should be large enough to be partially exposed above the water.

To make the stream appear to be natural, put in a variety of plants along the water's edge that are indigenous to the area. The banks will be almost more appealing than mother nature's if you select and arrange an assortment of six to ten types of plants that will eventually mature into a potpourri of colors, shapes, heights, and sizes. The easiest plants to care for, which are also the fastest growing for most climates, are bamboo, tufted grasses, ferns, Japanese maples, and rushes. Check with a water-horticulture expert for those that will not impair the ecosystem you are establishing.

If you have a passion for nature but also delight in the unexpected, create a stream that offers all that is natural yet presents a surprise or two. In place of large rocks indigenous to the area, try using several different sizes of flat stone or slate. Dry-stack the stones on top of each other to create a ledge for

unusual types of rocks are combined unnaturally, the rocks become a distraction rather than an enhancement.

To add even more of a surprise to your new water feature, cover small strategically placed sections of the stream's bottom with polished rocks, pieces of worn sea glass, and other treasures such as large glass spheres. Select these items in shades of blue, green, and purple, so that when clear water flows over them the colors will make the water appear infinitely deep. The entire streambed doesn't need to be covered with these specialty items; the expense would be prohibitive for most of us anyway. Simply choose a few areas approximately two feet in from the water's edge. The accents that can be placed in your stream are only limited by your imagination.

Try putting a large Japanese lantern in a spot at the top of a cascade, where the ivy or ferns have taken over. Or you can cover a section of the streambed in a collection of shells, all of one kind or each different. The insides of shells, such as abalone with its opalescent quality, make watery depths especially lovely.

Place a chair or bench close to these special water features so that others can rest in quiet comfort and enjoy them. Ideally, the path that travels by your stream  should be made of complementary materials and it should meander in a direction following the flow of the water.

the water to cascade over. Different types of rocks can be used, but make certain they are all in the same color range and are dense enough to handle the rush of the water and constant submersion without becoming dislodged or destroyed. Certain types of slate, for example, will crumble over time. Use rocks in all shades of red, gray, black, or tan. If colors are mixed or

Chapter 8

Lighting

*N*ature's sunlight is perhaps the most volatile and misunderstood of garden elements. It ebbs and wanes, as do the tides, from morning until the moon comes out. It moves around the garden with the seasons. We recognize its importance as a catalyst for the photosynthesis process vital to the growth of garden plants. We plan our activities around the light, and we use it to set a mood. Light is powerful. Light must be planned for, controlled when necessary, and supported electrically when there isn't enough of it. Light is as important for successful gardens as water, healthy soil, and appropriate plants. No master plan for a garden should proceed to the implementation phase without a careful study of light requirements and enhancement possibilities.

It is easy to get caught up in the excitement of planting a new garden and forget about its technical underpinnings. Such considerations include wiring for light, sound, running pumps, fans, heaters, and hot tubs; installing electrical outlets; and putting in gas lines to fireplaces, grills, and lantern poles. These garden features require preparation and should be included in the comprehensive plan for the landscape as well as the project budget. By putting thought into these aspects of the infrastructure, comfortable enjoyment of the outdoors from morning through night and into the colder seasons will be assured. Basic to the underpinning plan is cleverly disguising all wiring components and the noise they make. Plan for how you will be able to access them for turning gas and electric power on and off and to perform necessary maintenance. Though hiding electrical junction boxes in shrubbery is a simple solution, working under sticky rose bushes is naturally something we want to avoid. Imaginative homeowners and garden designers have thus ingeniously used rocks, birdhouses, and garden containers as places to conceal electrical boxes.

Light makes after-dark magic happen in the garden. Auxiliary lighting is a basic requirement for appreciating the aesthetics of the garden in the evening. It is essential for increasing safety along stairways, bridges, and paths, as well as around swimming pools and other potential hazards. For example, the lighting along a stair wall can come from above the climbers as well as a spot at the level of their feet, particularly where missing a step could send someone tumbling into a swimming pool. Safety concerns here are crucial.

However, too much light can be as detrimental to a garden setting as too little. Assess the needs of each of the garden areas and the people who will use them for a variety of activities. For example, a lighted tennis court adjacent to a romantic shelter allows spectators in both areas to enjoy the game. But if the glare of lights, perfect for picking a moving tennis ball out of the night sky, makes the gazebo guests feel as if they're sipping champagne in a parking lot, the spill light is overkill. Concerns such as this point to the need for planning lighting solutions as carefully as gardeners select their plants. Often times, subtle is best. The light from a fireplace or candlelight on a deck is probably sufficient, whereas nearby activities should be fully illuminated. Flexibility is important in your electrical lighting and power-source planning.

Making certain that outdoor electrical systems are not all on one wiring circuit will make it possible to switch off lights and equipment in one area while another is supplied with power. Multiple circuits will also help prevent power overloads. Simple dimmer switches are excellent solutions for creating special mood effects.

The model for lighting the garden isn't Yankee Stadium. Outdoor lighting should not appear harsh or contrived. Achieve drama for focal and transition points by subtle and selective high-lighting. Do not underestimate the beauty of creating interesting shadow patterns and silhouettes, as well as more direct lighting effects. The structure of pergolas, lattice, openwork railings and fences, filigree gates, and gingerbread embellishments, all create intriguing shadows.

Such elements cast their shadows in natural sunlight during the day; but at night their dramatic impact needs to be controlled with the careful placement of artificial lighting. Direct and ambient lighting can play up the focal-point and activity features of your garden, including sculpture, ornamental trees, wall art, fountains, waterfalls, gazebos, and pergolas, as well as your outdoor kitchen. In these cases, not only does the light help us see, but also the shadows that are cast add to our appreciation of the garden. Spill light from wall openings should thus become an important consideration in your plan.

Light designed in concert with movement is often overlooked as an outdoor enhancement.

Light and resulting shadow patterns create excitement, especially when they are in motion. In a garden area where guests are lingering over a meal, use subtle illumination to take advantage of lacy foliage that rustles in the slightest breeze. The same sensory rhythms can be orchestrated for wind chimes, whose theme shapes can dance with music, light, and shadow. Use paddle fans to help create these moving shadow patterns. The flowing movement and splash of fountains, as another example, beg for enhancing light that sparkles on their water surfaces. Play light and shadow silhouettes purposefully against rock walls, stone floors, entryways, and textured ceilings for visual delights at every eye level. Plan for interestingly lit low areas that are peaceful and serene, which we can view from above on decks, bridges, and terraces.

As the natural light moves across the garden (above), the shadow patterns cast by branches, lattice, and wrought-iron plant supports create a feeling of movement.

Be aware of eye-line levels within the entire garden. Visualize how light from below, to the side, and up high, as well as direct or indirect light, can be exploited for maximum comfort, surprise, and delight. Lighting-design experts emphasize architectural details, decorative accents, and foliage in ways that may not have occurred to you.

Study their ideas in garden magazines and books, or consult a local professional. As with a pathway map, it is advisable to make a design layout of natural lighting by times of day and year for where the garden receives full sunlight, partial shade, or moonlight. Then the plan for support with direct and ambient lighting by means of gas or electric units will become clear to you. Include in your plan reflected light from expanses of water, panes of glass, and mirrors, which you can manipulate for dramatic effect.

Fortunately, technology and imagination can combine to solve the stickiest of challenges in outdoor lighting. We've moved well beyond the porch ceiling light fixture and stringing colored lights around the roofline at holiday time. Many of the most successful solutions to dimly lit side-yard entries, swimming-pool cabanas, and stairs that climb through wooded areas have been conceived by imaginative homeowners. Architects and landscape designers are pioneering new ways to exploit industrial lighting technologies and products for private-property use. Artists and crafts enthusiasts are getting into the spirit of innovation with ideas of their own. They transform found objects, recycled treasures, and materials usually used inside the home to create lighting fixtures and illuminated garden art. Often whimsical, their results are nevertheless practical and uniquely expressive of their personalities and artistic taste. Yours can be, too.

Harnessing light to do what we want it to do takes discernment as well as electrical expertise. Assessing needs early is vital to the design concept in terms of elevation and location. Delightfully, when we combine imagination and improved illumination technology, light can do far more than help plants grow and keep us from tripping over a stone in the pathway. Effective lighting not only improves the comfort and safety level in our lives, it also adds to the beauty of the environment in enchanting and ever changing ways.

Sunshine and shadow move across the garden from morning to evening, illuminating and shading each feature in turn. It is amazing how transforming man-made lighting can be on the same garden once the sun has gone down. Good garden lighting design combines architectural and water features with landscaping into a special and highly satisfying outdoor atmosphere. Not only is the garden comfortable and inviting, but also every texture and pattern are distinctly accented. Electric light from above sparkles on water fountains and ponds, and when the water is lit from below there is a glimmer effect. Shadow shapes at night create a sense of magic nonexistent during the daytime.

In the garden shown here (left and above), though we view the same setting from different vantage points, the contrast between natural daylight and man-made evening light is dramatic. It plays up the pond enhanced by an unusual in-water fountain feature and natural rocks lit as pleasing foils for blooming plants.

Note how each of these elements, as well as the umbrella-table arrangement on the patio, appear to be features in an entirely different garden. The carefully orchestrated lighting designed for nighttime is the key to the totally altered look in this garden between night and day.

Chapter 9

Garden Furniture

The epitome of outdoor comfort is having a great place to sit or recline. To decide on furniture for the garden, think first about locations offering pleasing views. Then select furniture in keeping with the established garden theme perfect for solitude, an intimate conversation for two, and areas large enough for dining and other group activities. Your life-style and sense of aesthetics will determine the most appealing furniture pieces as well as their style and placement. Don't neglect considering little tables or stacked decorative collectibles that can serve as surfaces within easy reach of a comfortable chair. This way, a refreshing drink, a pair of binoculars for bird watching, or a good book is only the reach of an arm away.

Dining al fresco is a sensory pleasure for homeowners and their guests. Food tastes better outdoors, especially when lovely china, crystal stemware, and silver sparkle in the garden you have worked so hard to create. Tables should be large enough for comfort and must rest securely on the ground without rocking; otherwise, guests become uncomfortable for fear of tipping over their drinks. It's best to position tables where they are protected from the wind and at the same time afford an open view of the garden.

For an icebreaker setting, group several small tables with pairs of chairs to promote conversation. Unmatched chairs signal a casual atmosphere, so don't neglect this arrangement because you think you don't have enough of one kind of chair. Seating around each table should be comfortable enough that guests will stay to chat after dessert. Backless benches for picnics, on the other hand, do not offer that level of comfort.

Look for durable furniture, and if indoor storage is limited, choose pieces that can be covered in the rain or will be able to withstand year-round weather conditions. Wrought iron, treated wood, and painted wicker are charming outdoor-furniture material and style choices. Collectors of antique-period furniture, from rustic willow to enameled metal, enjoy mixing eclectic tables and chairs for a worn but shabby-chic style.

Each piece of furniture should express your family's life-style. Small occasional tables, arranged bistro style, can be placed in various areas around the garden. They invite a board game, a hobby, or a light meal at any time of day. Folding furniture is ideal for its ease of portability. Carry these pieces to an area where special flowers have just come into bloom, or perhaps a party requires a grouping of small tables in a certain area. Instant decorative embellishments such as baskets of ripe fruit and flats of blooming plants can add color and fragrance.

Children don't hesitate to drag cots and sleeping bags, blankets, and pillows outdoors for picnics and overnighters with friends. With this same type of spunk, cart a favorite chair, ottoman, or recliner to a special spot outside. Even if you have to use a wheelbarrow or a child's wagon to do it, your delight will be well worth the effort. Enjoy a book you've put off reading, with the sun dappling its pages and the chirping of birds close by.

What is appropriate outdoor furniture? The better question would be to ask what furniture would make you and your guests most comfortable in your garden for the season or a memorable afternoon. Leisure time is so precious, because it's often so hard to come by. Invest in your own need, not only to be comfortable, but also to feel pampered. Reward yourself for hours spent in an indoor office with restorative outdoor time in your favorite chair.

Benches, outdoor sofas, rockers, recliners, and gliders come in as many materials and designs as imagination allows. Consider their placement by how well they merge comfort, interesting views, and themes within specific spaces. Combine your choice of these furniture pieces in garden shelters, or clever and unique suggestions of them (below), to create inviting conversation areas. Place seating where fragrant blooms beckon visitors to pause and enjoy. Add a few throw pillows to sustain the comfort level, and bring on the iced beverages.

Seating along paths or within garden spaces encourages a more nature-involved perspective for visitors who venture away from the house and beyond the patio or deck. There, they can examine plants closely and savor their fragrances. The sounds of birds, moving water, and the notes of wind chimes draw visitors further out into the garden. With well-placed benches available at certain spots, they can pause to take in the restful beauty and harmony of nature.

Sometimes it is pleasant just to be alone in a comfortable outdoor rocker. There's something peaceful about the rocking motion and the creaking sounds that rockers often make. For times when we'd rather be involved with family activities, some hard-to-damage log stools and a rustic, sturdy table may just fit the bill. Consider the different swings available when imagining other nostalgic styles in garden furniture. Swings are perfect for quieting restless energy and reducing stress. There are various delightful forms from which to choose, from traditional wood-slat, wicker, or rope with a wooden seat to the tire swings that children love to whirl around in. Swings and gliders invite conversations for two and fit nicely on a narrow porch or deck.

Finally, it's important to have an area for the person who likes to nap or stretch out to read or daydream. Spaces for a reclining outdoor chair or chaise lounge should be away from the areas of high activity, with shade or partial shade, yet enough light for reading. The best hammocks are off by themselves in a grove of trees where the breezes come by. In planning the comfortable garden, areas for rest and solitude should be set off and separated by trees, shrubbery, or a low wall for greatest enjoyment.

Chapter 10

Garden Accents

*S*tatuary, birdbaths, bird feeders, lanterns, wind chimes, and candles all accessorize a garden to make it more interesting and personal. For placement, the same principles for designing interiors hold: create a focal point, coordinate around a theme, and accessorize to add interest or fill in spaces that are empty or so uniform that they lack appeal.

Garden accents can be especially exciting due to the greater latitude of scale possible outdoors. Imagine a twenty-foot-high kinesthetic sculpture surrounded by hummingbird gardens. A visitor to the garden can choose between enjoyment of the grandiose or the miniscule, or take in both simultaneously.

In the garden, a beautiful container, a statue, a birdbath, or a piece of sculpture draws our attention and anchors the spot in our mind. This spot becomes the focal point, in terms of design. The focal point offers a sense of place, which is important in having a feeling of belonging, and which in turn makes a space more comfortable.

Classical and formal designs are characterized by their symmetry, in which precisely balanced design elements are used. The focal point is determined primarily by the geometry of the space, and it is generally centered. The spot where you want to draw the greatest attention is marked with a dramatic plant, fountain, or sculpture serving as the focal point. To maintain symmetry, secondary pieces placed to each side of the focal point can be identical, similar, or of the same scale. The intention is to balance the mass, scale, intricacies, color, and texture so that neither side of the focal point dominates.

Achieving a truly classical formal garden similar to the great designs of the seventeenth and eighteenth centuries surpasses what most lovers of formal gardens aspire to these days. However, there are a few guidelines beyond geometrical symmetry worth knowing for a comfortable formal (versus natural) approach. Formal gardens integrate architectural and plant elements for beauty through order. This includes more rigidly defined borders, loggias versus decks, and the selection of classical materials like marble or other cut stone. Accents in the garden echo Greek and Roman columns and more detailed and lifelike statuary. Architectural finishes are highly detailed, and shrubbery tends to be very ornamental, often including topiaries.

Less formal spaces lack strict symmetry in determining the placement of the focal spot. With this approach, rely on interesting features that enhance a theme. Consider views that could be enhanced with decorative accents, outdoor "rooms," plays of light, and water features such as fountains.

Establish your focal point with an eye-catching item or grouping consistent with the feeling you want your garden to evoke. Other items you add to the space should support the theme but not overwhelm the focal point.

To accomplish a natural look to landscaping, garden accents should avoid looking contrived or rigid.

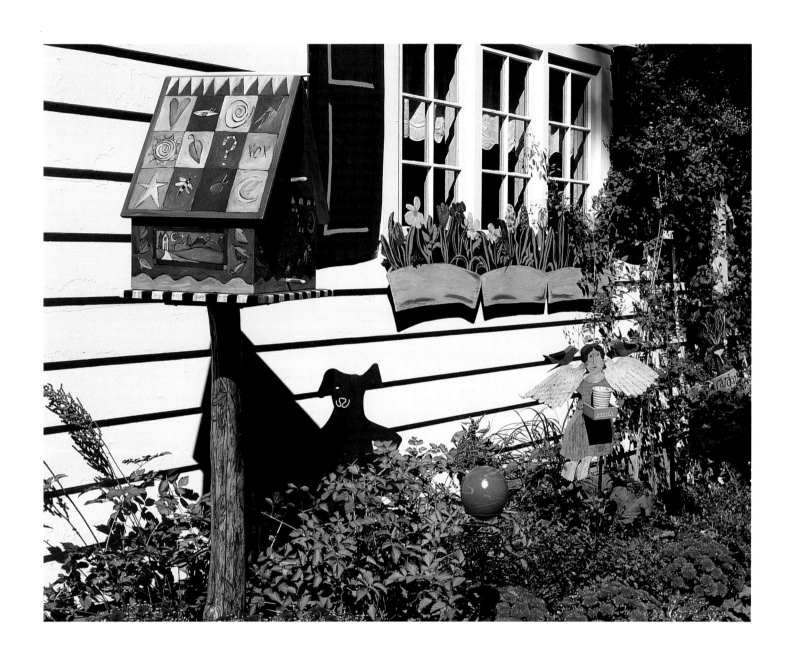

Some gardeners achieve an informal look by attempting to mimic nature's apparent chaotic placement and grouping of objects. Others select a focal point for the garden and then arrange everything else to support it. With informal gardens, symmetry and obvious planning are avoided. One of the attractions of this approach is that the garden can be changed easily for different looks every year. The focal point or points can remain the same, but the supporting garden elements can evolve and change with the whim of the gardener or the offerings of the season.

Informal or natural garden designs (above and right) can be humorous, whimsical, homey, or have an antique collectibles theme. All are casual, comfortable, and friendly. Many of these garden accents are hobby oriented.

Using what you have is one way of approaching natural gardening. Old tree stumps can be a true eyesore in a garden, but this gardener decided to make the most of what could not be changed. He hollowed out a section of the tree stump, filled it with soil, and planted beautiful flowers there. The flowers are planted densely so that there are no bare spots, and they can be changed with the seasons. These flowers and their container fit just fine with the scheme of the house and the rest of the garden.

It's been said that if selecting and growing plants is the heart of gardening, adding accessories or decorations is the soul. The garden art you choose tells all who visit who you are, what you love, and what type of atmosphere you are trying to create in your garden. Formal sculpture, a stone fountain, handmade containers for flowers, vintage birdbaths, or rustic outdoor furniture in the right place can add a sense of permanence, create a certain ambience, and fulfill our needs for comfort and belonging.

Whether you call it garden art, outdoor accessories, or just plain stuff, whatever you add to the flowers in your garden is the finishing touch. Collections that you have accumulated work well. With this approach, the theme can be anything that appeals to you. The sole prerequisites are that you love it, collect it, and want to use it in your garden. The items can be all the same theme, material, or color, have the same use, or be created by the same artist. The only thing that is important is that they are in good taste. Or you can take an alternative approach, using different items, as long as they, in one way or another, are expressions of yourself.

It is difficult to explain a feel for informal garden art, because there are no rules. For mysterious reasons, sometimes it really works and sometimes it really doesn't. Put what you want where you want, and if it feels right, leave it there. Rely on your gut feeling and intuition. One of the main characteristics of people who create informal gardens is that they are constantly adding, changing, and taking away accents. Part of the fun of collecting is that it is never finished. There is always one more thing, one more way to arrange the collection, and one more piece that just doesn't seem to fit anymore or of which you have tired. That is why these gardens are almost as interesting as Mother Nature herself. There is always change and the promise of something new.

A country-cottage theme calls for the nostalgic whimsy of a weathered chair and basket elements, an old water trough, and hollyhocks your grandmother would love. Add a family of metal bunnies just for fun.

Part of the allure of an informal garden is that it is a pleasing place to work. There is little more satisfying for anyone of any age than to work in the soil. To get your hands dirty, to plant something that will grow with the changing of the seasons, to pull weeds, to change things, is to enjoy all that any type of gardening has to offer on a sunny afternoon. However, with informal gardens, you can also use what is no longer useful inside, outdoors. An old chair becomes a planter, a cast-off brass bed is painted and literally becomes a "bed of roses," a series of kitchen pots and pans become containers for plants.

If you have a garden path that looks wonderful, fills the space, but is somehow lacking, place your favorite garden urn on one of the stones along the side. By adding informal garden art this way, you can complete a setting. In the end, the accessories you choose to enhance your garden become as much a part of the garden as the plants.

What is it that you want your garden to say about yourself? Our taste and sense of humor is sometimes easier to express in an informal garden than in words.

You may want your garden to send forth a quiet message of welcome. You may want to use something vintage in an unexpected way that states clearly who you are. Or you may prefer to make a bold statement, showing the world that you are assertive, love the unusual, and have a spirited side to your nature.

Whatever your unique personality, express it in your garden with an open mind and an open heart. It will bring joy and comfort not only to you, but also to everyone who shares your garden with you.

Chapter 11

Theme Gardens

*G*ardens designed around a theme have a particular appeal. Choosing a design theme can be much more specific than Mediterranean, contemporary, classic, or formal, for example. There are traditions for beautiful gardens in the Japanese and Chinese cultures, and desert-inspired low-water xeriscapes. You can create a theme that corresponds to the historical style or era of the home. There can be adaptations to regional conditions such as mountain rock gardens, displays around a color or a species of plant, indoor tropical gardens, or simply sheer preferences like cottage and water gardens.

One of the advantages in selecting a very specific theme is the focus and direction it provides in the design and choice of plants, features, and accents. Many creative people say that the more parameters limit them, the easier it is to narrow down to a creative solution. For a theme garden, the design considerations are the same as for any type of garden: creating balance, variation, scale, accents, paths, and enjoyable outdoor living spaces.

Asian gardens hold a fascination for many because of the way they evoke such a feeling of serenity and lend themselves to contemplation. Setting this theme is an invitation to learn more of the culture, plants, and traditions of those whom you are following. Graceful garden ornaments, lighting, and appropriate shelters further the theme, thus creating harmony in the environment.

Theme gardens in and representing the arid southwest are easy to enhance with sculpture, recycled-water features, decorative garden accents such as pottery and weaving, and materials like sand, gravel, adobe, rock, and sandstone, as well as succulent plants and cacti. The arid natural elements become part of the plan. You can create a space for comfortable relaxation by incorporating various components from the southwestern tradition. Tile roofs with deep overhangs, vegas, and rustic wooden doors should be included when designing garden shelters following this theme. If adding adobe-walled outbuildings, use a courtyard, loggia, or pergola arrangement on the property.

Xeriscape gardens, certainly the most arid of all, can be made even more dramatic than their spare beauty naturally affords with the careful use of pathways and natural materials. A path that leads to one stunning barrel cactus in full bloom is an experience to be treasured. Paths to such focal points reached by way of mounds of soil, sand, or river stone feel in keeping with such an earth-related theme.

The xeriscape garden is recognizable by its infinite textures, bold and simple forms, and earthy colors. Patterns in plant life make great silhouettes against adobe walls and raked sand. The harsh, dry prickliness of the native areas that suggest such a theme are so sculptural that they can be regarded as visual art in themselves.

For areas you will want to fill in with plants, tamarisk with its magenta plumes during its blooming season works well. It will take

over, however, so confining it will be necessary. The bulby seedpods of the wild creosote bush, as another example, appear like beads on its branched stems. We have all observed the eagerly awaited brilliant blossoms of the prickly pear cactus. Chameleon lizards with their own color patterns and ability to change their tones before your eyes are a theme-setting icon that can be found in sculpture, fabric, wind-chime shapes, and other decorative accents. Coyotes howling at the moon, roadrunners, and saguaro cacti are other easy-to-find images. They are available in collectibles, fabrics for outdoor furniture, and throw pillows that support the southwest theme.

High-desert and mountainous regions suggest themes for gardens that, whether austere and hardy or lush with stream-fed foliage, are ideal for landscaping in concert with nature.

Keeping within a theme often involves incorporating the existing mature trees, the most permanent plants, the elevations, and the structural walls into your design. For example, for a mountain garden theme, take advantage of rocky outcroppings, streambeds, inclines, and natural terraces, all of which can be played up for dramatic effect.

As high-atmosphere growing seasons are short, select plants with beautiful structured branches, so that once their leaves fall off, striking sculptural effects and silhouettes will continue to be interesting. Of course, evergreens are a good choice and their shallow root systems naturally acclimate to stony landscapes. These plants include boxwood, holly, bayberry, or sage.

Plan for the wind in canyon and peak areas. Plants as well as sculptures, fountains, containers, and decorative accents must be sturdy and well secured to endure the whims of nature. Because mountain soil can be rocky and thin, and the sun and wind often intense, the drying out of plants is a common concern. Take a tip from xeriscape enthusiasts and create rock arrangements as natural in appearance as possible. Then let nature supply the lichens and moss. Fill in any bare spots with rock plants, hardy geranium annuals, and plants in containers to add rich color.

Mass bloom varieties in banks of color on level ground or in terraced elevations (left) for an effective design plan borrowed from the past. Historic gardens with specific period accents from Europe's traditional eras often feature detailed statuary as focal-point art.

Recently, we've seen eclectic garden themes combining classical sculpture with antique collectibles, old tools, and aged furniture elements. With a timeless found-art appearance, such theme gardens can be charming.

The detailed carving of an animal, child, or angel with graceful wings and pose tells a story. It may be poignant or lighthearted, but it is rarely humorous. There is a tender sweetness about such sculptures that makes us pause to consider feelings, meaning, and beauty. Grouping these sculptures with fountains, birdbaths, and flowers that emphasize their themes calls for the placement of a bench for viewing.

The design of an historic home can inspire a theme, such as a Victorian garden. Through the design of the accents, planters, and walkways, you can further this theme and complement the decorative craftsmanship of the home. Keep in mind that designs influenced by an earlier period came from a time when comfort and ease within the garden did not receive the same consideration that they do today. When Victorian homes were built, there was an attitude of conquering nature and appreciating it abstractly at a distance. Today, we enjoy a sense of being part of the natural world. Therefore, traditional gardens for an historic home need some adjustments so that they are better suited for our modern attitude and life-style.

Themes can be very personal to us, especially when based around our collections. In this example, the garden holds the promise of a bird metropolis with birdbaths, sculptures, birdhouses, and feeders.

Establishing focal points and supporting them with detailed accents in keeping with the theme is essential. For example, when birds are the theme image, rabbits or fish, however charming, would be out of place.

Personal theme gardens provide display opportunities for those skilled at treasure hunting in thrift shops and antique stores, or creating beautiful items themselves. Gardens, patios, and decks are perfect places to exhibit creations, finds, and collections of these treasures, as long as they can withstand the natural elements. Collectibles bring a sense of surprise and delight to the garden as they do indoors. However, in the garden, they are often so unexpected that they are even more memorable there.

Acknowledgments

We would like to thank landscape designer Michael Glassman of Sacramento for sharing with us his views on comfort in the garden, and for supporting this project by including his designs.

This book is possible only because of the generosity of the many people who allowed us to visit and photograph their gardens. We are grateful to them for their many expressions of hospitality, and for the inspiration they offer others. We extend our thanks to:

Jim Pastrone	Jo Packham and Michael Rozzelle	Amy Adams
Linda and Chris Whelan	Maia and Peter Primgaard	Linda and Dave Durbano
Erika Akin	Jana and Fred Bartlit	Awleen and Ferris Keller
Lois and Grant Chappell	Carla and Charles Sigerseth	Cass and Jeff McNally
Judy and Gary Mangrum	Jeff Wright	Frances Savage
Manny and Debbie Carbahal	Sandy and Jim Figge	John Told
Tenley and Paul Coulter	Michael Glassman	Lynn and Doug Seus
Joan and Max Smith	Ellie Sonntag and Doug Stephens	Maggie and Ned Favero
Bob Jones	City of Salt Lake, Peace Garden	Mary and Eric Strain
Frances and Patrick Hays	City of Fresno, Woodward Park	Sara and Kelly Gardner
	Marla and Richard Ranney	

Credits

Brady Donley 68, 140

Chapelle, Ltd. 1, 6(bottom center), 7(bottom left), 7(bottom center right), 118(center)

Corbis Images (©1999, 2000) 11, 49, 107(top right), 170(bottom right)

Getty Photos (©1997-1999 PhotoDisc Inc.) 8(top), 9, 15, 18, 24, 25, 28, 32, 33, 37, 38(top), 38(bottom), 45, 47, 52, 53, 57(top), 57(bottom), 76, 81, 82(left), 90, 91(top left), 93, 97, 100, 101, 103, 115, 123(top left), 126(top right), 129, 130, 131, 133(left)

Jessie Walker 29, 40, 49, 118(left), 119, 121(top), 121(bottom), 122, 126(left), 127, 128(bottom)

Kevin Dilley 7(bottom center left), 13, 27, 39(left), 39(top right), 39(middle right), 39(bottom right), 58, 59, 64(right), 106, 107(top left), 117(top left), 117(right), 118(right)

Leslie Newman 17(right), 123(right)

Luciana Pampalone 19, 108

PhotoDisc, Inc. Images (© 1993, 1994, 1995, 1999, 2000) 4(top), 4(bottom), 5(bottom left), 6(bottom right), 7(top left), 7(top right), 8(bottom), 14(top), 14(bottom), 26, 30(bottom left), 36, 46(bottom), 54, 56, 80, 89(left), 91(bottom right), 111(top left), 111(top right), 112, 123(bottom left), 128(top), 138, 139

Robert Perron 31(top right), 62, 109(bottom left), 109(bottom right)

Index